Love, Life &

Legacy

by Akeem

Haynes

Love, Life & Legacy

Cover picture designed & drawn by: Simone Hayward

Cover Created by: Peter from bespokebookcovers

Edited by: Beverly Stevenson

Published by: Franchise Yourself Publishing

Bible passage & story taken from the holy bible, the new international version

Dedication

This book is dedicated to my Grandfather, Etel Samuels; though you are no longer with us I will always have you with me in my heart.

Acknowledgements

I would like to thank everyone who's been supporting me every step of the way. I truly appreciate those who have helped me get to where I am today. For that I am extremely grateful. I have to thank my mother for always finding a roof to put over my head no matter how hard it was at times. I've watched you grow up as a young lady to the woman that you are today. I may not have had much going on in my life, but you've always supported me and encouraged me to always reach for the stars. I would also like to thank Laurie and Alice. If it wasn't for those two women, I would not have been able to get as far in my studies as I did today. Thank you.

Table of Contents

Introduction

Anybody who knows me personally knows that I am a man of strong faith; during the bad times is when we need to hang on to our beliefs the most. Perfection is just a word; all we can do is try our best and make the best out of each situation. In my life I have been through a lot at an early age, but I've soaked up every single thing that I could and poured it into this book. I hope that when you read this book it moves you. I hope it uplifts your spirits and gives you an understanding that we are all together in this thing called life. We all have problems and a past but that doesn't mean we have to become slaves of negativity and the destruction around us. When you read this book, I hope it touches your heart and gives you that extra push to start doing whatever you want to do in this life. As I share parts of me in this book that no one would be able to guess. It's to show that life is what we make it, the beginning is never the final destination. God's plan is far greater than the ones we have for ourselves. I thank you for taking your time to read this, and I hope you enjoy it. God Bless.

When I think about hope and faith, I can't help but refer to the Book of Job in the Bible. This is one of my favorite stories in the Bible, and for those of you who do not know the story of Job, I would like to share it with you. Job was a man who was tested by God and through unyielding adversity he did not break. No matter how bad it was Job did not lose sight of what truly meant most to him, which was his faith in God. A man with undeniable faith is a man with many riches.

JOB

There was a man in the land of UZ, whose name was Job, and that man was blameless and upright, one who feared god and turned away from the evil. There were born to him seven sons and three daughters. He possessed 7,000 sheep, 3,000 camels, 500 yoke of oxen, and 500 female donkeys, and very many servants, so that this man was the greatest of the people of the east. His sons used to go and hold a feast in the house of each one on his day, and they would send and invite their three sisters to eat and drink with them. And when the days of the feast had run their course, Job would send and consecrate them, and he would rise early in the mornings and offer burnt offerings according to the number of them all. For Job said "It may be that my children have sinned, and cursed god in their hearts." Thus job did continually.

Satan Allowed To Test Job

Now there was a day when the sons of God came to present themselves before the Lord, and Satan also came among them. The lord said to Satan "From where have you come? " Satan answered the Lord and said, "From going to and fro on the earth, and from walking up and down it." And the Lord said to Satan, "Have you considered my servant Job, there is none like him on the earth, a blameless and upright man, who fears God and turns away evil?" Then Satan answered the Lord and said,

"Does Job fear God for no reason? Have you not put a hedge around him and his house and all that he has, on every side? You have blessed the work of his hands and his possessions have increased in the land. But stretch out your hand and touch all that he has, and he will curse you to your face." And the Lord said to Satan, "Behold, all that he has is in your hand, only against him do not stretch out your hand." So Satan went out from the presence of the lord.

Satan Takes Job's property and Children

Now there was a day when Job's sons and daughters were eating and drinking wine in their oldest brother's house. And there came a messenger to Job and said, " The oxen were plowing and the donkeys feeding inside them, and the Sabeans fell upon them and took them and struck down the servants with the edge of the sword, and I alone have escaped to tell you." While he was yet speaking, there came another and said, "The fire of God fell from the heaven and burned up the sheep and servants and consumed them, and I alone have escaped to tell you." While he was yet speaking, there came another and said, "The Chaldeans formed three groups and made a raid on the camels and took them and struck down the servants with the edge of the sword, and I alone have escaped to tell you. " While he was yet speaking, there came another and said," Your sons and daughters were eating and drinking wine in their oldest brother's house and behold, a great wind came across the wilderness and struck the four corners of the house, and it fell upon the young people and they are dead, and I alone have escaped to tell you." Then Job arose and tore his robe and shaved his head and fell on the ground and worshiped. And he said "Naked I came from my mother's womb, and naked shall I return. The Lord gave, and the Lord has taken away; blessed be the name of the Lord." In all this Job did not sin or charge God with wrong.

Satan Attacks Job's Health

Again there was a day when the sons of God came to present themselves before the Lord, and Satan also came among them to present himself before the Lord. And the Lord said to Satan, "From where have you come?" Satan answered the Lord and said, "From going to and fro on the earth, and from walking up and down it." And the Lord said to Satan, "Have you considered my servant Job, that there is none like him on the earth, a blameless and upright man, who fears God and turns away from evil? He still holds fast his integrity, although you incited me against him to destroy him without reason. "Then Satan answered the Lord and said, "Skin for skin! All that a man has he will give for his life. But stretch out your hand and touch his bone and his flesh, and he will curse you to your face." And the Lord said to Satan, "Behold, he is in your hand, only spare his life." So Satan went out from the presence of the Lord and struck Job with loathsome sores from the sole of his foot and the crown of his head. And he took a piece of broken pottery with which to scrape him-self while he sat in the ashes. Then his wife said to him, "Do you still hold fast your integrity? Curse God and die." But he said to her." You speak as one of the foolish women would speak. Shall we receive well from God, and shall we not receive evil?" In this entire time Job did not sin with his lips.

Part 1

"Sunny days wouldn't feel special if it wasn't for rain, Joy wouldn't feel so good if it wasn't for pain" - 50 cent

LIFE

Life is what you make it. You can wake up one day and everything that was there the day before might not be there tomorrow. Life is too short to live a life with limitations. Don't limit yourself because of your circumstances. It might not be ideal but that doesn't mean you can't make the best of it. Don't wait for life to pass you buy without making any effort to make something of yourself. The road won't be easy but the knowledge that you will gain through the ups and downs are lessons that you can't learn anywhere else. Spread your wings, and fly into a world of endless possibilities.

Chapter One - Separate Yourself

"*To be yourself in a world that is constantly trying to make you something else is the greatest accomplishment* "– **Ralph Emerson**

You can never be afraid to be different. Keep in mind that you already are, God made us each individually special and gifted.

Everybody is good at something it just takes some searching to find out what that something might be. Stand up for what you believe in, what you believe in is what will laminate your stamp in the world. You don't have to do what everyone else is doing, don't follow a crowd if you're meant to lead. Understand that you can't be copied there is no one like you, no one talks like you, looks exactly like you, acts the way you act, breaths the way you breath, smiles the way you smile, laughs the way you laugh, loves the way you love. NO ONE IS LIKE YOU. Don't change that, I challenge you to be different in a world where they tell you that acting outside of the box is unacceptable. You might think differently but that doesn't make you any less significant. You are you, and no one else can do you better than you!

Writing Your Own Chapters

You might be down today and maybe even feel like not getting up out of the bed, but don't let the process have you doubting yourself. In most cases things are going to get worse before it gets good. There is a book for almost every single thing except life. Every day you have a chance to write your own pages and chapters. Remember your book is written in pen, so if you're going to make a mistake make sure you get something out of that mistake. You only get one book but more than enough pages to make your book a best seller, however, you can't create a best seller if you sit around having an attitude because things aren't going your way. Life is what you make and every time you wake up with air in your lungs you can make it a good day. Don't expect to be helped up if you can't help yourself, you don't get out of life what you think you deserve. Nobody is going to just hand you what you want and the sooner you stop hoping for that to happen the sooner you will set yourself on the right track. You don't need a hand out from people, you will never know your full potential until you can make some good things happen yourself, don't be afraid to fail. After failure comes success! Control what you can control and don't stress about what you can't.

Disappointments & Failure's

2010 was probably one of the most challenging years of my life, but at the same time, it taught me how to endure and appreciate what I have instead of taking it for granted, especially the little things because they are the most valuable asset. The little things consist of being able to wake up daily, having a roof over my head, clothes on my back and surrounded with people who want to see me make something of myself. It's the little things we often overlook. It all started on the track. I was having a very successful indoor season, I was tied for #1 in the world in the 60m for U-17 and it stayed that way the whole year. During my very last indoor meet in Pocatello, Idaho I felt my hamstring grab slightly during the race, but by the time I felt it, I had already crossed the finish line. However, little did I know this was a sign that would affect me in the long-run. Unfortunately, it turns out that the little grab turned into a tedious injury. As a consequence, I pulled my hamstring in my very first meet outdoors in California. For those who don't know what a hamstring injury is, a hamstring injury occurs when you strain or pull one of your hamstring muscles – the group of three muscles that run along the back of your thigh. It makes the smallest things like walking painful, depending on how severe it is. I returned home and for the next few days the feeling of sadness and hopelessness crossed my mind often and frequently. It's hard to find motivation to try and get back healthy when you're in pain doing everyday routines as simple as lying down or sitting down a certain way. I began watching TV for long periods of hours; I had even lost my appetite. When you're an athlete and you get injured it's heart-breaking because all the work you have put into the season is now put on hold, and time isn't waiting on you to get back to being healthy. I started to feel pity for myself. Asking myself questions expecting to receive no answers back, those questions like "Why? Why did this happen? Why me?" When you're facing something that you don't have the answers to, you have to understand that maybe at that particular moment that there is no answer to the question, you just need to get through it. Often times we look for clarity to make us feel better, but sometimes you just have to take it for what it is and move on, and that's what I did. Eventually I picked myself up and started a five month rehab process that not only tested me physically but mentally, as well. It started off with simple activities like stretching, then I moved on to walking on the treadmill, then on the stationary bike and after about two months, we started doing more vigorous activities like running on the treadmill, box jumps, small strides on the grass, but every time I felt some sort of discomfort or pain, I would get into a daze of lost hope and then the next day I would remind myself of the little things I should be thankful for and I would then find that hope to continue again. My routine during the rehab process consisted of waking up at 6AM in the morning, rehab for about an hour, then coming home to shower and head to school. I was never a person to sit down for anything especially an injury, but this time, I had to be patient. I was trying to get back in time to run track for my last year of high school, and then in the summer the plan was to make the World Junior Team and compete for my country at home. It was something that my coaches and I had been thinking about for over a year. That was the goal. Unfortunately, that goal didn't come to life. In the last race of the day during the 4x100m relay during our high school championships, I pulled my hamstring again. This time I wasn't able to walk off the track, I collapsed on the ground losing control of the baton. Not only did I reinjure myself but we didn't get the win that day. Until this day, that's what hurts me the most. We were defending champions, I was very close with those three guys on my team, and I wanted nothing more than to end high school the same as when we came in, as champions. When you want something so badly and it doesn't' happen the way you expected it too, it makes you feel empty, but I knew that wasn't the last opportunity I would get to run track. I knew I would continue to run, I just didn't know where that would be. Nonetheless, I was ready to start the next chapter of my life. I never thought in my wildest dreams that I would get the opportunity to attend school in the U.S. and do something I enjoyed, as well as getting my education, not because it was something that was impossible but because it was something I never thought about, leaving my mom with my brother who was just born. At the time it didn't seem like it would be feasible, but yet that opportunity became a reality. I was getting recruited for two different sports, football and track, and they were all offering full ride scholarships; I didn't know much about American schools, all I knew was that it was an opportunity to get a free education and compete at a high level. However, there were steps to take and those steps included taking a test I knew nothing about.

While I was in rehabilitation for my track injury, I started getting ready for the S.A.T. exam; The SAT was short for Scholastic Aptitude Test. I didn't know much about the test other than it tested in three different categories, writing, critical reading and mathematics, and apparently I needed to take it. My physical education teacher took me out of phys-ed classes, so that I could study and get ready for the test. We found an old SAT prep book that had a bunch of practice test questions, and that is what I would work on instead of participating in phys-ed. This went on for a whole month, five times a week, and then sometimes a couple hours on the weekend. I would study this book and go over questions after questions, problems after problems, until it was time to actually take the dreaded S.A.T. I remember the first time that I took it. I answered every single question, not knowing that points could be taken off for the wrong answer. Needless to say, the result was far from what I needed. My spirits weren't shot though, I figured out what I needed to do, and, in fact, it made me much more motivated to come back and do better the next time. The next time I took it, I improved, but it wasn't close to what I needed. I had done better on each section but I struggled with math and that was my downfall. I ended up taking that test two more times, including the A.C.T which stood for American College Testing, and I still didn't get the score I needed. At that point I had nothing left, I didn't feel the need to waste any more time on a test that seemed to have my number each time I took it. I tried and tried and tried and received nothing from it. I'll be the first to admit that I am horrible in math, but I tried to fix that. I got with a math teacher at my school and each day she would go over a whole section of problems with me and show me how it's done step by step. But for some reason when it was time for the test I blanked out. Not only was I defeated, I felt stupid, and when I spoke to some of my other friends who took the same test and they scored almost 500 plus more points than I did and referred to it as easy, and I couldn't agree with them because it wasn't easy , at least not for me. I began struggling with confidence and started doubting myself, "Could I really make it in college?", "How did I graduate high school?" These were some of the thoughts circling in my head. Prior to the exams, I had taken pride in myself, my knowledge and learning, and when I couldn't apply it to one test, I felt feeble-minded. But I trusted God's plan for me and I knew there was another option. I didn't get the Test scores that I needed to be eligible to go division one but I soon realized, even if I did get the test score that I needed, I couldn't go because I later found out that one of the math classes that I took in high school, the NCAA didn't accept anymore, automatically, ruling me ineligible. That night I prayed and asked God to help me out and give me a sign that something good was going to come out of this, any sign. That sign I asked for appeared right before my eyes. About a week or so later another opportunity came into my hands. Barton Community College, a Junior College in Great Bend, Kansas was offering me a scholarship to come to their school. Without even taking a visit or speaking to the coach on the phone, I knew that this was a sign, a second chance to correct my wrongs and for that I had to take it. I was going to make the best out of the situation and never look back and keep moving forward. With my school problem finally being resolved, I couldn't help but think about that day when the injury occurred, even though I was healthy now, I was still not as sharp as I was before. Earlier I spoke about dropping the baton in the 4x100m relay and injuring my-self, but what I failed to elaborate on was the fact that I knew something was going to go wrong that day. That day of the high school championships as I walked off the bus at the track, I looked up into the skies and they were sort of grey and the energy I felt didn't seem right to me, my train of thought reverted back to ,a time when my mom told me "If something doesn't feel right, then don't fight it go with your intuition, live to fight another day". Nonetheless, I was very optimistic. I had successfully completed all my individual events and even though my times weren't as good as the year before I defended both my 100m and 200m title. All that was left was the 4x100m relay. Before the race even started, as I stood at the anchor spot which is the last runner who gets the baton, I looked up at the skies once more and I said to myself, "Whatever lesson you're about to teach me Lord, please give me strength" Bang! The gun went off and the race began, my team was losing which was strange because we were always ahead after our second exchange, except this time. I watched as one of the teams handed off the baton before we did. As I got the baton I knew in my mind that I was not ready to go as fast as I needed to, but at that point it wasn't about me, it was about the team. So I took off and caught the guy in front of me, but a few meters before I passed him, I felt my hamstring grab, and I tried to push through until I couldn't push anymore. The last thing I remembered was collapsing on the ground and hearing the crowed gasping. The baton flew in the air as I rolled across the finish line. The next thing I knew a woman was asking me where the pain was. I knew something was going to happen, I could feel it the moment I woke up that day. My year was finished, when it came to running, again that year. The main goal of making the World Junior Team was out of the question now. Those same thoughts I had five months ago when I started the rehab process were coming back stronger than they were before. Except this time my heart was feeling extra heavy. A few days after the meet, one of my childhood friends passed away. He was stabbed four times at a party. I was truly at a low point, and I started to expect bad things to always happen to me and affect those people around me. I remember going to dinner with Mr. Rose, who throughout my high school days, was basically my mentor. I remember asking him if he believed in curses. He looked at me and paused and finally said, " No, and I hope you don't think you are either." See, at the time, I didn't know what to think, I've always been told that hard work is supposed to pay off, but it didn't. I did everything that I was supposed to do on and off the track, it was supposed to come together, and when it didn't, I couldn't quite grasp the implications, clearly. Until one day when I was taking my little brother to the park, and as I held his hand and he looked innocently at his surroundings, smiling and touching everything he could get his hands on, I thought to myself, "here is a kid who's a year and a half and he's so happy just being outside and enjoying the walk and we haven't reached the destination yet", and that's when I realized that bad things are inevitable, they're going to happen, but it's how you respond to it that shows your character. No matter how many times you've been knocked down, you have to get back up, life will continue to move, you can either move with it or you will disappear. You don't have to be the brightest or smartest or fastest or strongest person to be significant. There's unlimited potential inside of each and every one of us. The most important things are what we often overlook; we lose sight of the little things because were so focused on the big picture. But it's the little things we should cherish the most. The goal is the finished product, but without taking the small steps and making mistakes, we won't truly appreciate how far we've come. When you have failed at something try not to take it to the heart, in the grand scheme of things it's just another way of reminding yourself that you have to regroup and look at it through a different angle. When you've been wrong and been down so many times, eventually you will put together the correct pieces to the puzzle. No matter what you go through, no matter how hard it is, think of the little things that made you want to change your life. Small changes completed well make big things happen correctly. Even though that year didn't go the way I wanted it to, I was still grateful for what I had learned and what was yet to come. I was more determined to make the following year my best year. I realized that life isn't a fairytale story, nothing's perfect nor will it ever be, giving up won't get you any closer to where you say you want to be, and often times you have to go through some experiences to see how bad you want what you desire. Defeat is not the worst of failures, not having tried is as bad as it gets. And as far as failure, itself, is concerned, you're not obligated to keep trying; all you can do is your best every day, that's all; and you're always good enough to do that.

Faith

Maintaining faith through tough times is the ultimate test. When you work hard for something and you don't get what you want, it's easy to get unfocused and give up. But you can't. Faith is believing that no matter what happens to you, you're going to find a way to keep pushing and prosper from it. Faith is believing that *nothing* can turn into *something*. Faith is like planting a tree. When you plant a tree, you can't do much but water it and make sure the area is clear so it can grow. At the beginning this process is exciting because you can envision how big the tree is going to be and your plans for that tree. You are optimistic because, in your imagination, you already see the possibilities for your tree. Even though you can't physically see what's going on underground, yet you know that day-by-day the tree is growing, slowly but it's growing. Eventually you will go in and out of that excitement feeling because it's taking too much time to grow, and throughout that time, things may fall on top of the seed you planted, it might be rocks, or garbage or leaves. However, the thing about the tree is that it doesn't matter what happens around it. As long as you keep watering it and let nature do the rest, the tree is going to find a way to grow around or over the garbage or rocks; it's definitely going to grow. The point is that whatever you believe in, whatever you want to achieve, you have to plant your seed in it and never lose hope, always maintain a clear vision of what you want. No matter how cloudy it might be, after the storm comes along, the rainbow appears.

Pride

Don't let your pride keep you in a box to which you don't have the key to. What I mean is don't think to highly of yourself because of what you've achieved or what you've done. Don't be too close-minded or one-sided that when people are trying to help you, you brush them off and you ignore them. Pride only breeds quarrels, but wisdom is found in those who take advice. Be thankful for everything you have because as quickly as everything comes, it can go just as quickly. Always be true to yourself and never forget that at one point you started with nothing. Keep the base you learned at the bottom because a solid base builds an efficient working foundation.

Chapter Two - Finding the Light in the Darkness

When facing the darkest of times, this is when you are tested the most. This is when you need to dig deep into your faith and believe that everything will work out. You can't stay stuck in the darkness, once you get complacent in staying in the dark the fight is over, it means you given up and thrown in the towel. That's one thing you can't do, you must keep fighting, you must get back up, and you must dry your tears and find a way to keep moving. It's hard, it's dang near impossible to pick yourself up when nothing seems to make sense. When all your confidence is gone, what you need to do is start thinking of the smallest things that are going well for you, remember that when you were a baby for the first few days or weeks you couldn't really see very clearly, but you trusted that the people around you would take care of you. True faith comes from being stuck in the dark and believing that one day the light will find its way in because you've found a way to keep fighting when it was easier to give up. DARKNESS CAN'T AFFECT YOU IF YOU

BELEIVE THAT YOU ARE THE LIGHT TO YOUR

OWN HAPPINESS.

Resentment

When you hold on to pain caused by other people,

you engrave that person in your head. As much as

you want them out of your life there're stuck there

because you refuse to let it go. You can only hold in

your anger for so long before you blow up, and in

most cases you blow up on the people that care

about you the most. Yes it sucks to be hurt or

betrayed, but what good do you get from lashing

out on those who are trying to help. The only way

to truly get the power back in your life is to forgive

them, not for their sake, but for your own peace of

mind. Ask yourself, do you truly want to be

happy? Or suffer and never get back a piece of you.

Do what you're Passionate about

If you are passionate about something, pursue it, no matter what anyone else thinks. Whatever makes you happy, excited, and continuously intrigues you is what you need to hold onto. Your passion for what you love to do is what's going to elevate you on your journey to complete happiness. A lot of people are stuck doing things they hate doing. We all want to be financially stable, but when you hate doing something it becomes a burden instead of enjoyment. Sometimes the richest people have the most problems, because they put up a mirage, meaning that from the outside it looks like everything is great, but once you get closer and dig deeper and deeper you see that nothing is truly as it seems. Most things are not always as smooth sailing as they are perceived. Make sure in this life you always do what you love. You only have one life to live.

Strength

You are stronger now than you once were; you are smarter now than you once were; you are a better person now than you once were. True strength comes from overcoming what people did not expect of you. Often times we feel that when we are vulnerable that we have become weak, but then you are able to wipe away your tears and decide that you are going to make a change. When you learn from past experiences, it takes you to a new chapter in your book of life, and as you start a new chapter, you learn how to get past the moment when you felt vulnerable. Then you can use your weakness and turn it into something you can use to make improvements within yourself. This shows that you're growing. Strength doesn't have a time line or age limit, it's something that we develop through experiences. Sometimes people think to be strong is to never feel pain. In reality it's the strongest people who feel it, understand it, and accept it. Every time you feel a little shaky, repeat to yourself, "I am stronger now than I once was, and I can't be broken, I am strong"

Fear

In 10th grade, I remember One day I was walking home from school, I could either take the alley or walk all the way around. Of course, I was going to take the alley because it was a shorter distance, so as I was walking through the alley, half way through I heard a loud barking sound, and the next thing I knew, I looked left and saw a dog running towards me from a connecting alley. Immediately I turned and started running and didn't look back. Fear is like a dog, it's going to come after you, it's going to make you scared and make you panic because when it comes around, it expects you to surrender to it, but you don't have to give in, I outran that dog with my backpack on. After that experience, I told myself I would never take the alley again. But, for whatever reason, my instincts prompted me to continue to take the alley. When I would see that dog again, I would take off running. It might not have been the smartest move, but in life, you can't be afraid of anything. All you need to do is punch back when fear punches you. Eventually you will be so stubborn that fear becomes nothing but just another word.

Chapter Three –

Insecurities

This is one thing that kills most people. We all compare ourselves to everybody else and that's something you can't do. When God created us, he gave us all a different purpose in life. A person's life may seem like glitter and gold, but nothing is truly as it seems. We are all fighting similar battles, you might think you're going through a situation alone, but you're not. When I was younger, I was chubby even though I was very active playing sports, and because of that, I became very self-conscious about my body. It seemed like no matter what I did, I still couldn't lose the stomach. I'm not afraid to admit it, even until this day that I'm uncomfortable to some extent, but each day I become more comfortable in my own skin. For this reason, it's important to "Be confident In Yourself". You matter beyond belief. Don't get caught up in the public's society of what a person is supposed to look like. They look a certain way and so do you. There are no duplicates of you; you are the only model. Why would you want to ruin that by being someone else? Authenticity is much more potent than a copy right, don't get distracted by bringing somebody else's vision in your head. Insecurities kills all that is beautiful and unique within you.

Trust

This is one of the hardest virtues. You can't trust everybody; everybody doesn't have your best interests in mind. Be careful to whom you expose yourself too because those same people will hurt you if they feel like it will help them get above you. Sadly, you can't trust everybody, even the ones who say they are with you, for words mean nothing without the actions behind them. Trusting someone with your heart may leave you vulnerable and maybe even make you feel naked, but sometimes risks are meant to be taken. If you can't open up to someone then you will be trapped in a world that will make you feel alone. The loneliest walk you can take is the one by yourself. I'm not saying you shouldn't trust, but be careful who you let into your circle and life, if they aren't adding value to it, then you need to subtract them from it.

Support

Not everybody is rooting for you in this world, some people want to see you do well, some just say that but don't want to see you do better than them, or even reach half the goals you set out for yourself. I always think that out of everybody that you know, there are probably about a handful that will support you no matter what. Anybody can be supportive when things are going well but their loyalty shows when you're down and out. Sometimes the ones you're closest to are the ones who will try and snake you and break you down when you least expect it. You have to be careful with whom you share parts of your life with. I learned that at an early age. Anybody can hurt you, even your own family. I'm not saying you shouldn't trust anybody or do everything alone because it's impossible to do everything yourself, but make sure who you put around you is on the same page as you. Put people who are just as hungry as you are, people who are going to pick you up when you fall, people who are generally great people all around, ask yourself, "if everything was supposed to fall apart at this very moment who would be the ones still here to support me?" If you have a hard time answering this question, then you already know the answer. And if you're in that boat, it's time to re-evaluate your surroundings and get the right people around you. Success sometimes changes people, don't be the person who changes for the worst and forget the ones who have been there for you since day one. Don't get so caught up in your own success that you forget that the ones around you have goals as well, As much as you want to achieve yourself, be sure to help them reach theirs as well. I think of a support team like a basketball team. On a basketball team you have five on the court. Your point guard is the one who makes sure everyone stays on the same page and reassures the players that there is more than one route to take in order to get to the main goal; the shooting guard is the one who always has a plethora of ideas. Whether it's dumb or brilliant, any idea is better than no idea. It means you're trying and you always need someone that's optimistic through everything. Shooting guards take the most shots so you need one of those people who won't give up because they go 3-20 from the field. A small forward is one who can see the future, one who gets an idea and runs with it,

whether you're covered or in open space you see
an idea and you can make the best of it at any given
time. A power forward is important because you
need someone to help set screens for you, someone
who will help you get over the roadblocks and
questions the situation because you don't have
answers, like a "pick and roll". The team can help
each other. Sometimes you have that person that
you talk with differently than any others, whether
it's on a personal level, or you need advice or just
need a pick me up, and usually power forwards are
good for that. And last, but not least, you need a
center. A center is the best rebounder. In life,
nothing ever really goes as smooth as you
anticipate. Sometimes when your back is against
the wall and you fall down, at times you need
someone to help pick you back up and get you in

the right direction. Someone who won't give up on you, someone who understands that you're human but still encourages you to keep moving because brighter days are ahead and this is the value your center brings. These are the kinds of people you need on your team, now, if you have them in your life, you need to be grateful and thank them. You are fortunate because not too many people have people like this in their lives; it's hard to find genuine good human beings. When something is genuine, it's not forced, never forget your true supporters, they will never lose faith in you.

Procrastination

There is no such thing as procrastinating; you make time for what you want to get done. When it's a priority, it gets done, when it's not, it gets pushed to the back. Have you ever noticed that when your teacher assigns you a paper to write, you start your paper depending on when the due date is? If it's due in a few days, it gets started right away, but if it's due in a month or two, you will start it later. Whatever task that you have, understand that the sooner you get finished, the sooner you can check it off and start something new or even get ahead. When you want to achieve the things you say you want, it's important that you get started now. Your dreams won't wait. Either start now or sit and watch someone else achieve their dreams, you don't get what you wish for you get what you fight for. Successful people use every single second that they have, they know how valuable time is. Use your time wisely. We can't get back what we have wasted. Time is a precious luxury.

Hope

Every question that we have doesn't always have an answer. When we first start out, most things that we are searching for aren't always intended to be found. But that doesn't mean we should stop the search, don't stop looking or growing, even though we may seem lost at times. It's not always a bad thing. You can find yourself through the darkest of times, you can begin the process of mending what was once broken. Don't let anybody dim your light with thoughts of hopelessness, you've been down before yet you've always found a way to get back up, to pull through. You're better today because you made a choice yesterday that enough was enough, no matter how hard it may seem we must never lose hope.

Overcoming Adversity

Sometimes the hardest thing is trying to keep yourself from breaking down when the going gets tough. Adversity has no remorse for the way you feel, it will kick you and step on you when you're on the ground. No matter how much you're hurting adversity is going to keep applying the pressure on you. Through every hardship you have to maintain faith and trust in what God is preparing to send your way. There's been plenty of times where I've been one worse break away from completely breaking down, but the constant stubborn attitude of being overly optimistic has kept me going, and kept me believing in God's plans. God might not answer all our prayers right away, but He leaves clues, He sends the support we need through people to help us up when we're down. Success will never be easy but always have faith in yourself and the possibility of what can be and if you are persistent in achieving your goals, soon enough it will become reality. Think of it this way, if you always get what you want, when you want it; would you be as strong and resilient as you are now? Probably not, these are the lessons we need in life. Embrace the many mistakes you've made along the way, and use your past mistakes in today's lessons. Don't be ashamed of what you've been through, no one has a perfect story, imperfection is a beautiful thing, it shows that even the strongest people are human.

Three Quick Ways to Turn a Negative into a Positive

1 - Just Breathe

Honestly in most cases sometimes you just need to stop and think about the situation. Is it really that serious? I used to let the smallest things get under my skin and I used to spend most of my days aggravated until I truly slowed myself down and thought about it. We can never control what people do or say towards us, but we can control how we react.

2 - Controlling Your Thoughts

The mind is unspoken words without structure; if you can change your attitude from the inside then your body language will follow. Too many times we forget that we have a choice to act or feel a certain way, nothing is truly ever permanent.

3 - Don't Fall apart

When things start to go downhill, consider that it is happening for a reason, not to bully you or to punish you, but to get you ready to build something bigger than the situation at hand, something that suits your personality and reminds you that you have to keep pushing and searching until you figure out your purpose. Sometimes things fall apart so better things can fall together; it's one of the many gifs of life

Embrace the good or bad that life throws at you, because in the end it is a learning process. Life has a funny way of working itself out in the end if you believe that everything will be okay, and if it's not

okay then the battle is still undecided, and if you

keep fighting, You can still win!

Part Two

"Spread love everywhere you go. Let no one ever come to you without leaving happier " - Mother Teresa

LOVE

Love is one of the most powerful emotions in this world. It makes us feel a way that sometimes words can't describe it, and that feeling is something we have to experience. There are those who think that they are incapable of loving and that's definitely not the case. Love is amazing when the two involved are flowing with the current and not fighting it. When it's right that feeling will sneak up and surprise you, before people get married how do they know that a particular person is the one? I'm not entirely sure because it's something we have to go through when the time is right. Love is a beautiful thing, and that is why we need to spread our love. Love is at its greatest strength when shared.

Chapter Four- Stay True To Yourself

One of the hardest things to do is staying yourself in a world that wants you to be like everybody else. Nowadays there is so much that says, "Dress like this, you should be this complexion. You need this." No, you don't need any of that. "Nobody knows you like you do. One of the greatest gifts we have is the power to think and act for ourselves.

Never think that you have to be like everybody else and why would you? You were made for your own purpose, you can't do what your friend does and they can't do what you do. All you can do is respect their opinions or anybody's opinion and keep it moving with your own life. The only person that has the right to critique yourself is you. Never forget who you are and where you came from. The morals that you've learned growing up are what you need to refer too when you feel lost. Remember nobody can do a thing like you do it. You are powerful beyond measures. Say it, Believe it. Act like it.

Friendship

The word friend is something you can't toss around on a regular basis, because everybody isn't your friend. A true friend is someone who is going to tell you when you're wrong no matter if it causes an argument, a true friend is someone who fights the currents with you, a true friend is someone who is going to be there through the bad times and actually mean what they say. And, often there is a misunderstanding between following through your words and just saying it because it sounds right. Everything sounds right until it's time to actually show it. At times, I've had people tell me all types of good things but have yet to follow through with what they say. However, there was a time when I was away at school and I spoke to my mom earlier in the day and she was telling me how there was no food in the house, and how tight money was. As soon as she told me that I called on a few people back home who I could count to help in the situation. Because I wasn't there to help and barely

had any money myself to send to my mother, God

planted the right people in my life to help my

family. A friend is someone who acts first when

you need them and then asks why later. You don't

need someone in your life who isn't going to

consistently be a friend. Nobody needs someone in

their life who's going to show up when they choose

too, and if that's the case, I wouldn't want that

person to stay anyway. Never force anyone in your

life who isn't planning to stay in the first place; be

careful who you bring into your circle of friends,

don't ignore the signs when they are so clear on

what their intentions are. Some people will use you

to get what they want and then leave without

hesitation. Make sure you pay attention; a true

friend will never let you go through any situation alone, especially when you need them the most.

Don't Push Away Someone Who's Trying

When you give your time to someone who doesn't respect you, you surrender pieces of your heart that you will never get back, all failed relationships hurt, but losing someone who doesn't appreciate and respect you is a big plus, not a negative. Some people come into your life temporarily, simply to teach you something. Sometimes people come into your live to get you ready for the next person. Unfortunately, sometimes that's just how it is. Nonetheless, they come and go and they make a difference. Don't be bitter about your past if it didn't work out the way you wanted it to. Don't carry luggage with you that you should have let go when that door became closed. Because when you say there isn't any good men or woman left, how do you expect to find a good one when you've subconsciously blocked them out? Of course, when a good one reaches out to you on a genuine level sometimes, they are considered "thirsty" why? Because you're not used to being treated like you claim you should be, and that scares you and you push them away. Nobody wants to ever feel vulnerable, to risk getting themselves into a situation where they could potentially get hurt, who would want that?   But this is real life not a fairytale story, and, at some point, you must get over that, even a turtle comes out of its shell at some point. Remember pain is a temporary emotion and its offspring is love, they go hand in hand.

Swallow your pride

Apologizing doesn't always mean you're wrong, it just means you value your relationship more than an argument. Don't be too stubborn holding on to a disagreement. Life is too short for all that, no matter how much you love or care for someone, they will never be able to fully match up to the way you expect them to. They won't respond to your questions like you think they should, they might, but most of the time they won't. You are two different individuals. This is what needs to be understood. They don't have to agree with you all the time, don't pout or get angry with them, its fine. Be willing to compromise, sometimes it's not always about you. To make each other happy, the both of you have to be willing to make some sacrifices. For example, she might want you to watch the movie, The Notebook, with her; most guys don't want to watch a so-called chick-flick to begin with, but it's not exactly about the movie as much as it is that she wants to spend time with you. Even if you don't want to do it, do it any way, this will make her happy. These are the little things that females love. It's not all bad because you will benefit from this too, the next time you just want to sit down and play video games, she won't nag you about it. 9/10 if you give her the controller, she will play with you. Compromising is a key ingredient to a healthy relationship. You don't need to have a perfect relationship, but if you're willing to work at it, it can be molded into what you've always been dreaming about.

Consistency in a Relationship

People might forget what you did for them, but they will never forget how you made them feel. Whatever you did before you got in the relationship, to get your partner to be with you is what you, is what you must continue to do when you're in the relationship. If you would buy her flowers every once in a while, continue to buy her flowers once in a while. If you use to give him back massages continue to give him those. Don't change that, often times we get comfortable and forget the little things we used to do for our partners, and once you forget the little things, small arguments can potentially turn into big ones. Be sure to mean what you say, don't say something and then back out on it. Everything matters when you're in a relationship; it's about "us "not "me ". You should never change who you are but you have to be willing to make some adjustments. Especially if that person is worth it to you. Don't forget to be YOU AT ALL TIMES! He or she liked you when you were being yourself so don't change that. Consistency is everything!

Chivalry is not dead, or is it?

I always hear this saying, "Chivalry is dead." I do not agree. Chivalry isn't dead. People have just stopped requiring it. If you watch old movies from the 70's or 80's when a couple would go out to dinner, a gentleman would open the doors, push a woman's chair out until she sits down and then he would go around and sit down. In almost every movie that's how it would appear, and I'm not saying that doesn't go on nowadays because I'm sure it does, it's just not as appealing as it once was. You will be treated how you accept people to treat you. If you want someone to open the door for you, say so, but if you would rather open your own door, say so. If you want to be treated well, have respect for yourself and carry your name with pride and respect. Others will treat you as you present yourself, if you don't, then don't expect people to treat you well either. Those who respect themselves will be respected. Your name is your brand in this world and you have a duty to carry your brand with the upmost honor. A female can't expect to be taken seriously in a relationship if she is walking around half naked and going to the clubs every weekend. Likewise, a guy can't be taken seriously if he's trying to hook up with everything that moves. My mom always told me in patois "mek sure seh yuh nuh bring nuh sketel round ere ennuh, nah tell yuh again " which means whoever I bring around my mother has to respect herself, and respect herself enough to know what's right and what's wrong. Never forget your morals, and, in the end, those will never steer you wrong in the end.

Chapter Five- Baggage

This is inevitable; we all come with some sort of baggage from our past mistakes, which is fine. The problem starts when you try and bring your past baggage into your present life. If you have been treated unfairly in a previous relationship, you have to accept it for what it is; you can't bring the problems of your last relationship into your new one. Despite what is portrayed nowadays, everyone is different, there are still good people out there who actually value a relationship. It's not fair when you take out your problems on them. For example, I was talking to this girl for a while and I got to know her really well. We began to get extremely close and things were going well. Then, one day she told me that she needed time to think and that we needed to take a step back from a serious relationship. I was confused as to what I did or even said, it just didn't make sense. However, I respected her decision enough to give her the space she wanted and we didn't talk as much. A few months later I asked her what that was all about and she said, "I panicked, every time something goes well for me, something bad always happens and it screws up, I didn't want to mess this one up and I panicked and pushed you away.. I'm sorry." It was a logical explanation and we eventually worked it out and were able to move on. Sometimes you have to take chances. Nobody wants to feel stages of vulnerability and risk getting hurt but you can't be afraid totake chances. You have to let go of the past so you can grasp the goodness and the good people in the future. No relationship is a bad decision. If it doesn't work out, it teaches you what you don't want in a relationship, so set the bar for the standard that you keep for yourself, and if a person truly wants to be with you, your standards will be met. Trust me.

Leave the baggage in the past where it's supposed to be, everybody is different, your past relationships didn't work out for a reason, don't take it out on someone who's already accepted you for you who are and what you've been through. If you're stuck on the negative, the future may pass you by.

Torn Between the two

When you're blinded by love or infatuation you can do some foolish things without even knowing. You have to understand that not every relationship is going to last, that's just the reality of life. Sometimes we are often faced with asking ourselves questions like "should we stay or should we go ", even though the answer might be clear as day, it's hard to make your heart believe something your mind already knows. If you're hurting more when you're with that person and feel a sigh of relief when you're away from them, then that's something you need to take into consideration. There are things we don't want to happen but we have to accept, things we don' want to know but have to learn, and people we can't live without but have to let go; the decision is never easy but it's a part of life. At some point you have to say enough is enough and ease some of the stress off your heart, and remember that just because you love someone doesn't always mean it's meant to be. No one deserves to be unhappy with someone they care about, that's a battle they will never win.

Appreciation

We all want to be appreciated and feel loved. One of the reasons why relationships don't work out is because of unbalanced affection. There is no worse feeling than showing someone you care, and you don't receive the same care back, or when something is forced, nothing that is forced is going to be worth it. Nobody is too busy to show love to the ones that they care about. Life is way too short to hold in your feelings because you're "too busy ". That person might not be there much longer, no matter how much someone loves you or cares about you, everyone has their limit of feeling unappreciated. Once they feel unappreciated you can expect them to fall back and distance themselves, a heart can only take so much heat before it turns cold.

Get the Best Out OF Each other, Together

When you have someone in your life who helps you to be better in different ways, it makes you happy. Building a foundation from the ground up brings stability and gives you and understanding of what that person is about. If that person is there when you have nothing, then you have something special. Love can't be forced, it has to come naturally. It is like a flower, it's something that blossoms and grows over time, and it turns out beautifully if you let it happen when it's supposed to happen. It's not supposed to be perfect, but the individuals in the relationship need to be willing to give all that you have. Personally, I want something real based on effort, I need the actions to match the words. It's a good feeling when you have someone just as ambitious, just as hungry as you are for success by your side.

Offering More than Your Body

A mental connection has a far greater purpose than a physical attraction in the long run. It's good to have both but if you can only give your body than that doesn't say much. You have to be able to bring more to the table, there is nothing more attractive to me personally than a woman with goals and working towards those goals, a woman with ambition and self-confidence will only uplift you and add value to what she's worth. At a young age my mom and grandma made sure that I could do everything on my own (cook, clean, etc.) so that I wouldn't have to depend on a woman to do it for me. They also shared with me to be sure that she offers more than her physical flesh; if she can touch your mind then she has unlocked the door to your heart because she has now separated herself from the rest. To men, may I suggest that ladies aren't stupid, they want more for themselves. The same game that guys continue to run on them won't work with a woman who actually values her morals; a strong independent woman doesn't waste her time dealing with boys. If you want to approach a woman and not a girl you better get it right. The good ones are the ones who you have to be willing to work for. Gain her interest, get to know her, be genuine, and actually LISTEN TO HER. Ladies, let a man work to get your attention, make him rise to your standards. If he is truly interested, he will meet you where you set the bar

Five Stages of Red Flags

There are certain details we should pay attention to before we think about investing our time in someone, both for males and females, and this section will give you an idea of some details you need to watch out for beginning with the signs for the men.

"The Ex Talk"

Do not mention the "ex". Men, if you take her out on the first date and she mentions her ex, chances are he is still in the picture. If a person isn't relevant in today's society, why would she bring him up? Be careful with that one, if a person isn't ready to let go of past attachments, then she isn't ready to give her all to you and that will lead to an unstable relationship.

"Trust Issues"

Often times for females, the trust issue problems comes from within their own family. Most females, not all, but most of them who don't have a father-figure in their lives, have trust issues, but that doesn't mean they can't change and become someone you could be with. Just prepare to work that much harder to gain her trust and maintain this positive attribute of a healthy relationship.

"Club Girls"

There is nothing wrong with having fun and going out from time-to-time, but if you go to the club and you see the same girl there every time, that's a problem, it becomes an even bigger problem when you go to approach her only to find out that she's completely drunk screaming, " Turn up " Then maybe you should take that hint and turn right around and let that one go. A girl that parties 24/7 probably doesn't have much going on for herself and their trying to avoid the reality of that. And perhaps you ought to question why you are in the club so often.

"Inconsistency"

Here is an example. Females are usually by their phones, and if you text one and she doesn't text back, don't be naive thinking that she didn't get your text, she received it alright, she just decided not to acknowledge it. Inconsistency is the first sign to fall back

"So my mom/friend said"

First of all, the both of you are the ones trying to build something, not their friend and mother. There is nothing wrong with being close with them, but they shouldn't know everything, and if that's the case, this potential lady friend will have her friend or mother talking in her ear, in any decision that involves the two of you. It's okay to get opinions, but you want a woman who's going to think for herself.

Male Red Flags

"Slide in your DM guy"

Be careful who you talk to on social media, for example, if a guy messages you saying, " Hi stranger, you never text me anymore, what's up with that?" 9/10 what they noticed was the fact that you looked good in that last picture you posted and he is trying to "get to know you better " so don't be fooled. He might look good and might seem harmless, but that doesn't mean he won't flip the switch.

"I'll do it later"

Basically these types of guys are lazy and their priorities are out of whack. You can't simply do everything later, there's not enough time in the day to do every single thing you put off later. However, he can change and fix that habit, but you have to be willing to be patient and help him.

"The attention seeker"

These men are the ones who will look for any reason to bring themselves into the conversation. Usually they are loud, slight cocky and appear to have too much confidence, in fact, it is through the roof. You don't want to be with a guy who forces his need to be relevant. Behind the front, it usually means he has some sort of insecurities, and that can be a problem.

"The gossip guy"

Guys talk just as much as females these days, so, keeping that in mind, you don't want to be with someone who's going to repeat everything you say to him to his friends or your friends, like he's a parrot. Trust is earned, make him earn it. If men have to work for something, they will value it more. Once they value something then they will protect it by any means.

"Her? Were just friends"

That's not always the case, if the majority of a guy's friends are females, you might want to take that into play, and if a guy has nothing to hide, he will tell you the ones that matter from the get go, and he won't cover it up. I do believe that girls and guys can be just friends, just note the ones he omits to mention.

To both the ladies and the guys, these are some of the things you have to look at before you invest your time in someone. Don't rush being with someone who you are unsure of. Time is something you can't get back, and it would be nice if you didn't have to waste that on the wrong person.

Know Your Worth

Everybody wants something that's real, someone who's going to be here through the bad times not just the good times; you have to know your worth. Know that there is no such thing as temporary love, if they are changing everyday on you then you need to go, one minute there for you and the next they disappear, Either be there or don't. Nobody wants half of someone, don't make yourself miserable trying to please someone who isn't trying for you, don't rush something because the title connects better than the individual. If you find yourself constantly trying to prove your worth to someone else, you've already forgotten your value. It's a horrible feeling when you give your love to someone who doesn't know how to love back.

Chapter Six- Forgive When you're ready

When you touch a wound and it doesn't hurt. Then you know you have truly forgiven, of course those scars are still going to be there and you will have the memory that goes along with those scares, it reminds you of how it used to be, but once that wound is healed. It won't hurt anymore and no matter who tries to dig it up, it's fine because you've left it in the past where it should be. The past can't hurt you unless you let it, people are always going to bring up a situation that once hurt you, don't get sucked into the bitterness of a person who clearly has a problem with letting go. Instead you should smile and carry on, smile so big that they get annoyed. The reason why you can smile is because you have accepted the situation for what it is and moved on. Smile because you know walking away may hurt for a while, but your heart will eventually heal. Then you can choose what you really want.

The 100/100 Rule

That 50/50 meet me half way rule isn't to going to work. Why would you want half of someone? Or half their efforts, or half of their time, you have to be willing to go all in to make it work. If you give your best and your partner is giving their best, expect to see good things, expect to have a better chance of making it last. 50/50 is not going to bring you longevity. If the relationships didn't work out, you don't want to have thoughts doubting the amount of effort that you put in. Don't be the person saying I "could have done this, or should have done this ". Don't leave a void in your heart that you can't be filled. Leave everything on the table because a relationship requires work just like anything else. If you're willing to work to make it last, then you've done your part. Love is great when spoken, but greatest when shown.

Stop giving too many chances

You can only do your part. You can't force someone to give out the kind of love or put forth the effort that you give. Don't expect too much when they give so little. Don't be naïve letting those people who waste your time back in your life, thinking they will change. Let their actions interpret whether they have changed or not. They've had multiple chances and blew it, it's time to move on, and it's time to start putting yourself first for once. It has nothing to do with being selfish, it has everything to do with deciding that you are no longer going to put someone else's needs ahead of yours anymore. You can only make a mistake one time, after that it starts to become a choice. Your emotions are not something to be toyed with, so take some time to figure out if you want to dig yourself out of a hole. No one deserves to be miserable.

Trying to get it right

I've had a lot of my good friends go back and forth in relationships, they would break up with someone and then a few weeks later they were right back in the game. Then they would start dating again, and sure enough they would break up a few months later. For some odd reason when they would come to me for advice, they couldn't figure out why it never seemed to work out. As they would explain to me what's been happening, I noticed something that they failed to pick up on. They were dating the same kinds of people, sure physically they were different, but internally they were the exact same. I understand you like what you like, but if the same problem continues to occur frequently, what sense does it make to keep going back, trying to make it work? It's like travelling in a maze, you have to remember the corners and straights and turns that you take otherwise you will spend all night and day walking around the same route. You have to be willing to try something else, if it didn't work the first time or the second or the third time, chances are it will not prosper to anything else but a constant heartache. All failed relationships aren't always a bad thing because when it goes sour, it teaches you the things you don't want in a relationship as to when it goes well you remember the things you do like. Everyone wants to be loved and feel loved, but rushing to the next relationship after you just got out of one is not the move. Being single isn't always a bad thing, sometimes you have to take some time to work on you, figure out if your part of the problem. And if you're the one who's been hurt, you ought to sometimes take a step back and give your heart some time to heal and give your mind some time to gather its thoughts. You can only accept getting it wrong for so long before you give up hope. I know you're trying to get it right, so this time try a different approach and slow down and help yourself before attempting to make it work with another.

Heart break

There was a girl by the name of V, she was a college student at Baron University. She was very active in the campus community: she did shows to promote her sorority, she tutored many different classes, and she was also a law student. She was soft-spoken, loving, caring and you could tell that she just generally had a good heart. For as well put together as V was, her taste in men was not the greatest. At the time she was dating a guy named J, and they had been together for just over a year. On the outside looking in, J seemed like the ideal guy: he was funny, smart, worked out regularly, family-orientated, and overall, it seemed like the two were made for each other. However, it was not always as it seems. J was extremely controlling, it had to be his way or no other way and because of that, he and V would always buttheads and argue and fight, the worst part being that neither he nor she would admit that they were wrong. There was rarely any type of apologies shared between the two. One time J was waiting for V after class and she came out talking with a guy from her class. As soon as J saw her, he flipped out, "You know you shouldn't be talking to guys, are you dumb?" He scolded her right in front of the students walking in and out of the classroom. Lisa kept walking and said "Screw off J, get a life ". Things like this would happen on a regular basis, at least two-three times a week and it appeared that J was the one to act out. For some strange reason, V brushed it off and stayed with him even though this was reoccurring frequently. A few weeks later, V was speaking on campus about one of her projects on, "Subconscious Control." After she was finished, she was packing up her things and her papers slipped and fell out of her hands and scattered on the ground. "You made some good points today, I especially liked the one about empowering your thoughts." V turned around and looked up and said, "Thank you, the mind is a terrible thing to waste. " He replied, "That is very true. Hi, I'm T, what's your name? " In a soft voice she said, "V." "Very nice to meet you V. Would you like a hand with those?" He then reached down and helped her pick up her papers. V and T started seeing each other regularly on campus, they would wave and say hello and give some slight conversation before they continued their route to separate classes. The occasional time they would meet up and grab a quick lunch and that's where they would converse the most. V told him about her plans after she was to graduate, and she even told him about her relationship with J. For the most part, T just listened to whatever V wanted to say. He didn't mind listening to her talk. They became pretty good friends, and at the time that's all she saw in him. However, T was starting to have deeper feelings for Lisa each day. Meanwhile, J and V kept fighting, in fact, the fights got worse. One time they were supposed to go to the movies together, and he told her to meet him there because he was running late. So V headed to the movies for seven o'clock, which was when the movie started. She waited and waited until it was seven-thirty. She had been calling and texting J for thirty minutes, but yet she got no reply from him. Finally, she became fed up and left and still J was nowhere to be found. At twelve

in the morning, she heard someone knocking

at the door. She left her bed and went to open

the door. Little to her surprise it was J, and she

wasted no time in telling him off. She scolded

at him, "So you think it's fine to waste my time

and not answer my messages or calls?" J

began smiling and replied, "Whatever, can I

come in?" "Have you been drinking?" she

asked. Instead of meeting with V at the movie

theater, J had met up with some friends and

went out for some drinks, then his phone died

so he had no way of communicating with her.

Being the person who V was, she let him in

and they stayed the night together. She always

forgave him and tried to make it work, even

when he continuously messed up. The next day she met up with T, and in a rage as she told T about what happened with J the previous night. T had always been there for V, he would always go out of his way to do whatever to make her smile. One time she texted him saying she was having a horrible day. That same day he showed up to her house with a teddy bear and her favorite ice cream, and immediately her mood changed for the better. It was clear to see that T really liked her, every time they would hug he would hold her for longer than expected and he would joke about it after saying she smelled good which is why he didn't let her go so quickly. But the signs were there. He didn't do anything extra like try and kiss her or hold her hand or anything like that, even though his feelings were strong for her she was still off limits. In the end she still had J as a boyfriend and T didn't want to come between that out of respect for V and her relationship. Later, on a particular day V and J were having by far their biggest argument. One thing led to another and J slipped up, grabbed her, pushed her on the couch and she fell and hit her head on the table. J didn't even feel an ounce of remorse, he just stormed out and left V crying to herself. Later that day she called T and asked if they could meet up and talk and he said of course. They met up a few minutes later and the first thing he noticed was her puffy face and red eyes. Instantly he knew that she had been crying over something. "What happened? "He asked. She told him about the argument and how J had put his hands on her and pushed her and that's when T stood up and said, "Leave him, you can't stay with him, "and she replied, "I know but...:" "V let me take care of you," he said. V looked at him and replied, "Wait... What? You? I didn't even know you felt like that about me." That moment every emotion that T was holding inside came out " V I have been in love with you since the first time I met you that day, I helped you pick up your papers off the ground. Every second I'm away from you I want to call and just hear your voice, but I stop myself because I know it's not my place to do that. You ever wonder why every time I hug you I hold on so tightly? Or when you would talk and I would just listen to your every word? Everything that you've ever told me is imprinted in my head, and I want to know everything about you. That is why I just listen to you. I know more about you than your so- called boyfriend does, I know for a fact that he can't treat you better than I can treat you." Lisa was shocked! She didn't expect anything like that from T. "Be with me, "he reiterated. " I can't" she stated, "I still love J, I'm sorry" and she walked away leaving T by himself. T tried to call V later that night and then the next day, and the next day, but she didn't answer his calls or reply to his texts. A full month has passed by and one day V saw T walking to class and she ran up so that she could catch up with him. As she got closer, she tapped him on the shoulder and he turned around and she started talking. "I know I haven't replied to your calls or texts, but I've been going through a lot and I was confused as to what to do, I'm done with J for good." "That's good," he replied and he began to walk away, but she ran up to him again and said, " I'm ready to be with you, I've been doing some thinking and you were right, I want us to be together and try and make it work. I'm sorry that I've been so blind. I know I did you wrong, but I know this is what's meant to happen." T smiled and said. "Be with me? You don't get it do you? I've been trying to call you for weeks trying to see if you were okay, but you blew me off. I understand you were confused, but I wanted to go through that with you, I knew you were scared, but so was I. You never thought about me did you?" " I did, "she stated. "No, no you didn't, it's not always about you, a small piece of me wanted to wait for you, but an even bigger piece of me told me that I deserved better, I needed to move on, so that's what I'm doing," he replied. Lisa was distraught and looked puzzled and hurt, she didn't expect it to go this way. " I came here looking for you to apologize for my wrong-doing and you' re brushing me off like there is nothing between us?" "Now you can see something between us? I would have walked a million miles to get to you, but you didn't see that did you? Of course you didn't. That day you came to me to talk, I poured my heart out to you, and it went against everything I stood for, I made a promise to myself that I would never come between someone who was in a relationship, but I risked that because I loved you, and sometimes when you love someone, you have to act on your heart and not what your mind is telling you. You claim to be hurt but do you really know? Ever poured your heart out to someone not to get an answer back? No? Let me show you. "T put back on his headphones and walked away leaving Lisa staring blankly into his direction.

Three key tips to stop doing

One

Stop wanting someone who doesn't want you back; you're wasting your time chasing someone who has no intentions of being caught. Save yourself the stress and the mind games.

Two

Stop rushing into commitment. A wrong relationship will make you feel more alone than when you were single. Don't get infatuated by the title if you're still having doubts about what you want. It's better to take your time and be sure than to rush and get hurt or possibly hurt someone.

Three

Giving someone too many chances will leave you continuously angry and bring you more pain. Don't make excuses for someone who isn't trying as much as you are. You get out what you put in, it's a shame when you put in more and get nothing out of it.

It's about growing together even at the darkest of times, your partner wants to know that even when things look shaky you're not going around messing with others who have no business being in the picture, We all want something that's secure, something that no matter what happens you still know that's " Yours" at the end of the day. We don't want perfect, we just want something that's real.

Part Three

"The things you do for yourself are gone when you are gone, but the things you do for others remain as your Legacy" –

Kalu Kalu

LEGACY

When your name is mentioned, how do you want to be remembered? How will your last name be used in context? The reason why we are able to remember guys like Steve Jobs, Albert Einstein, Isaac Newton, Martin Luther King, is because they created something that would last. They believed that what they did would make a difference in the world, they knew their impact on the world was bigger than themselves. What's your legacy going to be? How can you impact the world?

Chapter Seven -Stop making excuses

I understand that there is a reason for what path a person takes, life is hard. Something's are harder to explain than others, and it makes you do things you never thought or even imagined you would do. However, remember that it does not have to become your only option. I always made jokes with my mom telling her that I raised myself and she didn't raise me. When I would say this, she would reply, " Oh yeah? Raise yourself out of this house then," and we would start laughing and that's how it would end. In this statement, I realized that I did raise myself for a majority of my life, no disrespect

to my mom, she raised me the best she could but

she wasn't always there and that was not her fault.

Throughout my time high school before she

became pregant, I didn't see my mom very much.

My mother worked two to three jobs, and I'd see

her mostly on Saturdays and Sundays. Until this

day I'm still not sure how she did it. Most days as I

was going to school she would just be coming in

from her night shift, and as I arrived home she

would just be leaving to start the process all over

again. For years people have asked me how I kept

everything so tightly wrapped, and the truth is I

didn't do it for me, I did it for my mother. I didn't

like seeing her slave herself to make ends meet,

living from cheque-to-cheque. I could have done

anything I wanted do. School didn't have to

become an option. I could have had parties and leave the house as many times as I pleased, but that was not the path I wanted to take. Seeing my mother work so much it taught me that I had to be that much more responsible for myself. I wouldn't change that whole process if I could because everyone has to grow up at some time in their life, my time just came a little earlier than most. I always hear stories about how kids deal with their parents getting a divorce. At that young age it made them do some crazy things. I had a friend who I witnessed going through the process. At first, he started drinking daily, he skipped school, went from being an honor student to failing almost every class. I remember one day after football practice, walking home I passed by his house and decided to check in on him. We sat and talked for hours, and while we were talking, he said to me, "Akeem, how do you make yourself happy? Can we actually be happy or is it just something we chase but can't catch it?" At first, in my head, I didn't know why he was asking me that particular question, but I understood he was emotionally unstable. As I thought about the question, I replied "Well man, I don't think a person can chase happiness. We have it in our hands, so doesn't matter where you are or what happens because we have the power to create our own happiness. Each day, instead of complaining about the things that are wrong in our lives and the things we don't have, if we can adjust our thinking in our heads, small changes will start to happen. Think of the little things going well. All we need is a spark to remind us that what we have is more than enough." He kind of just stared at me and then stared at the ground, then he smiled and made a joke. There and then he realized that, even though his parents were getting a divorce it wasn't the end of the world, and he was still going to see them both and that was better than nothing. You have to make the best of the situations around you, they might not be ideal but that doesn't mean you can't tolerate them. It might be bad but it could always be worse, don't use an excuse to go down a road that wasn't intended for you.

Letting Go Of The Past

The past is the past, and you can't change it by thinking about it all the time. You have to let go of the past and anything negative in your life before you can really be ready to be happy. Your past has made you what you are today, but it's not the end product. You have the ability to create your own future, but if you're holding on to pain, grudges, and heartache from the past YOU WILL NOT GROW INTO WHO YOU CAN BE. Let go of the things you can't control, let go of a situation you can't change, don't stay stuck in regret when the present has already forgiven you, let go of thinking there is such thing as perfection. You are human, we all are, everyone makes mistakes, but it's what you can learn from those mistakes that makes life worth living. It's like learning a new math equation, there are many different ways to find the answer, but there are usually short-cuts to save you time and still get the correct answer. When the teacher is showing you a new format to answer the question, they show you new steps to solve the problem, a way that's more efficient and effective, and if you revert back to your old habits, it will take you a lot longer to solve the problem. You will eventually get to where you want to go in life; it's on you whether you get there motivated by happiness or molded by anger.

Changing the Way You Think

There has been many times in my life where I would think that the worst is always going to happen. I would think that things would never work out the way I wanted it to, no matter how hard I worked for it something would always come to ruin my joy, and in my head, that's how it would be because that's how it's always been. As I got older, I realized that things won't always go the way you want it to go. You don't get out of life what you think you deserve, you get out of life what you work for and maintaining a positive mindset through the bad times. We were all brought up differently, and, in most cases, we become products of our own environment. Sometimes we forget that we have the power to control our environment. As you get older, you don't have to do something you don't want to do. Don't be afraid to make your own mistakes, mistakes help you grow and it's one of the best learning experiences you can get. Learning is important when life is the teacher, you have to believe that you're going to be successful, put it in your head that each day you're going to do something that will make you better for the next day. Have faith and believe that one day your time will come.

Nothing Is Truly Permanent

Don't get caught up thinking that bad things are always going to happen to you. It might seem like it might continue to be that way but remember you have the power to change that. There was a time in my life that I thought I was cursed because I couldn't catch a break, when one thing happened, another bad thing would happen right after that and I truly struggled with thinking positive thoughts. I told myself that I couldn't keep thinking like this, I had to break this cycle, so I began to start thinking like an optimist, even when I didn't believe it right away I would fake it until I believed. Eventually those negative thoughts were at a minimum. A lot of the emotions that we have won't last, it might hurt or affect us for a few days, or weeks but eventually in time that feeling will subside and that void will be filled. Every successful person has doubted themselves at one point or another, they, too, were afraid to fail, but they wanted to succeed more than they cared about failing and that is where their strength came from. True strength comes from following your heart when your mind won't co-operate.

Being grateful

We spend so much time complaining about the things we don't have, and then when we get what we want, we complain about something else that's missing and we continue to ask for more, neglecting the good things we have going on already. The only way for good and new things to come into your life is by accepting and being thankful for what you have. Life is not like a payroll where you are guaranteed something, in fact, you're not guaranteed a thing, and that alone should make you appreciate what you have that much more. If you're stuck in a rut of some sort, it's easy to get fed up and let negative thoughts in, but all that does is help you take steps backwards. Not only are you stuck, but now you've put these thoughts in your head, which makes you think that your time will never come. Add that with the frustration, and your mind starts telling you things you shouldn't be listening to. Once you lose your own voice, you lose sight of what kept you together. Yes things might be bad, but they haven't completely taken a turn for the worst. I always say when facing hard times, God is testing your faith in him. How can you not believe in someone who's given his life for yours? No matter what you are going through remember that things could change in a matter of seconds, remember the story of Job to which I referred to at the beginning of this book. Here is a man that was faithful to God's words yet everything he had was taken from him and yet he did not break. Happiness doesn't come from materialistic substances, it comes from being appreciative and thankful for all that you've been blessed with.

A Lion's Mentality

Lions by far is my favorite animal, and the reason why is because of the way their mannerisms are presented. A lion goes around the jungle knowing he owns the place. The thicker a lion's mane is the more power he has in the jungle. Likewise, when you walk with confidence your demeanor changes. A lion doesn't worry about anything other than providing for its family. It doesn't get distracted worrying about another animal. The difference between a lion and most animals is the hunt. When a lion hunts, he is not just hunting for himself, but, day in and day out, he is faced with the ultimate ultimatum. If he doesn't catch his pray the family doesn't eat. When he hunts, it does it with a purpose. He puts everything he has into catching his pray. In a similar way, when you feel like quitting and don't think you can possibly take another step forward, remember the reason why you do what you do is because people are depending on you. All they want to know is that you are out there doing your absolute best, and if you know you're not doing your best, don't feel bad when the results come back and your plate is empty. The lion has no choice but to succeed. Tap into your lion's mentality and start preparing your plate today!

Chapter Eight- One More Rep

When my brother was about one or two years old, I would hold his hand and bring him over to the dirty laundry basket and dump his clothes in the basket and I would repeat this with him every day. When we first started out, he didn't get it, I would come home from school and his clothes would be everywhere but the laundry basket. I knew I had to be patient with him, so I repeated the same routine, and finally one day, I watched him take off his clothes as he got ready for a bath and put his dirty clothes into the basket. When he did that ecstatic. We had repeated that same routine so many times and to see him do it once was well worth the reps we did for this one moment. It might seem like sometimes we are just going through the motions, and we might be, but when you feel that way think about how rewarding it will be once you've achieved your goal. It's like walking in the desert and you're ridiculously thirsty, and tired and you just feel like you're going to collapse if you continue any longer. The heat from walking so much has completely drained you, you have no energy left to continue walking. But from a far you can see a glimpse of what looks like water and for a second you get excited again about the possibility of getting to the water, and you have now just caught your second wind. All you have to do now is keep taking one step at a time moving forward. And eventually you will make your way to the water that you saw from a distance. No rep is a waste of time. With every rep it brings you a step closer to where you want to be.

Going All In

After coming off an injury in 2010, using 2011 to work my way back and 2012 being an

Olympic year, I knew the only way to make something positive happen was to go all in. My coach came and picked me up from the airport and I told him that I had to run fast, there was no if ands or buts. I had to get on that Olympic team and he told me, "You will get there, let's work." My coach at Barton College was a very relaxed guy, but, at the same time, he was demanding. I truly enjoyed being coached by him. That year I made a lot of sacrifices: I ate much better, not that I ate bad to begin with, I watched videos, and I'm not the biggest fan of watching videos of track, so I don't do it as much as other track athletes probably do but. nonetheless, I watched when I could, I didn't go out, no parties for me, and every Saturday I would get up at 6AM and head to the track to do drills and small exercises that would help me in races. Then I would head back to my room and sleep until 9AM and then get up and head to the gym to get another workout in. I was fully locked in, my mind was so focused that I couldn't be broken. Even when I had a bad race, the next one would be better and I believed it would be. When you go all in, you have to be willing to give up the past, so you can be ready to dive into what could be and what can be. You can't be satisfied with yourself because once you"re satisfied then you get comfortable, and once you're comfortable, you let your guard down, and once you let your guard down, you invite all types of negativity through the door, and just like that, you could stumble if you don't catch yourself. When you're locked in and you're in your zone, the only person who can get you out of that mode is you. Be willing to go all in for your dreams. If you have a job interview, make sure you're practicing talking in front of the mirror. GO ALL IN. If you're trying to lose weight, do not eat what everybody else is eating. Don't cheat yourself. GO ALL IN! Don't commit to something if you're going to quit half way through. Follow through. It doesn't matter what it is, at the end of the day actions get results. I ended up making the Canadian Olympic team that year; I learned that if you want something you have to go all in, you can't be a half-ass success. Make a

choice today that you're going to GO ALL IN!

Subconscious Thinking

The mind plays so many tricks on us that we

over think and over analyze the smallest

details which makes us stressed. We add

worries that have no right to be there in the

first place. It's like getting an injury, say for

example, pulling your hamstrings. Once you

hurt it, it's always going to be in the back of

your mind, no matter if it's a slight pain. That

small pain has now escaladed twice as much,

but now that you're thinking about it, you're

going to be that more attentive in your next move. It's like when you watch a scary movie and you know it's not real, but your friends hype it to be something more than it actually is, and because they did that, it gets into your head, so now when you go home, you're paranoid. Every time you hear a sound, you think someone is in the house, but your doors and windows are locked, your mind is playing tricks on you because, for a split second, you believed that there is something making those noises. You subconsciously have created an image in your head. Sometimes you have to just have to take a deep breath and tell your mind to calm down. As much positive as you can think, you can overlap those thoughts with one thought of self-doubt. The mind works how you want it to, if you don't expect good things to happen to you, they never will, but if you do expect good things to come your way, then they probably will. What you seek is what you will find, what you think about can be molded into your reality.

It's the Little Things That Count

Starting something is the hardest part of the process, the end will come together when it's supposed too, but if you don't start correctly, your empire will fall. You can't ignore the inevitable, skipping steps will hurt you more than it will benefit you. You have to ask yourself, do you want temporary success or longevity of success? John Wooden, a former basketball coach at UCLA, used to show his athletes how too properly tie their shoes and how to wear their socks, so that they wouldn't get blisters because blisters can lead to bumps and bumps can lead to discomfort and discomfort can lead to possible injuries. When you're focused entirely on the big picture, you lose sight of the small steps you have to take to get there. That's why you can never get too excited and think too far ahead. I always hear students say, "I can't wait till Friday "or "TGIF". The problem with this sayings is that you still have to deal with

Monday, Tuesday, Wednesday, and Thursday you still have regular classes and things to get done, you still have school to attend. You can't move ahead to the next day if you don't take care of the present day. If you use the full potential out of each day, you won't need to say "today sucks "you will be excited to seize the following day because of what you were able to accomplish the day before. Each day gets a little easier; if you develop a routine that works for you, those long days won't start to drag. If you know you have a busy week ahead of you, plan accordingly over the weekend; create an agenda that gives you an idea of where you can use your time. It's small but it's effective. It's the patterns, Consistency of the little things that develops success.

Fight for Your Dream

When you have something in your head and in your heart that you want to achieve, you have to protect that with everything you have. People are always going to try and knock you down when you have already fallen. Don't lose sight of what's in your head no matter what happens, Never forget what your dream looks like and the steps you have to take to get there. Don't expect anyone to believe in your dreams, ITS YOURS not theirs. Don't expect pity from anyone when you continuously fall on your face, and don't expect to be helped up if you're not willing to help yourself up first. They don't have to believe in your dreams for it to come alive. It's never going to get easier; nothing is going to be handed to you. You have to fight for every single opportunity, and when you don't have an opportunity, sometimes you have to create your own opportunity, put yourself in the right place, don't expect support for a dream that only you can see. In the end it will be worth it because you gave everything you had into an image that was once only in your head. Very few people actually have the guts to even attempt to start doing the thoughts in their heads. Make your dream a reality. Even if you don't succeed, the fact that you attempted to go after what you want shows that you are fearless. Failure is a part of success. Once you have that fearless mentality... what can stop you?

"It's tough when things don't go your way, it's tough when you don't get what you want. But to never struggle is to never grow" –Akeem Haynes

The Janitor's Lesson

Every day after our morning weights session, I
would go over to our academic building and do
any work that I had before class. I would always go
up to the third floor because it was quite. Every
time that I was up there I would bump into this
janitor and I would say hi and he would ask me
how I was and then I continued on my way. For
three months the same thing happened every day,
and every day he was more and more enthused as
he was cleaning. I said to myself that, this guy had
a lot of energy, he was always so responsive and
always smiled when he spoke with people and I
admired that because with his line of work, it's

easy to get grumpy and stay that way. Cleaning up after college kids is not my idea of fun. One day I decided to find out more about this guy. I was very curious, so I asked him what his name was and he told me, and I told him my name. He asked me what my major was and what sport I played and the small things like that. I had a question in my head that I wanted to ask, but I wasn't sure how to ask because I didn't want to offend him. Eventually I found the courage to ask him. I said, "Mr. E I don't mean to sound rude or come off as that but I couldn't help but wonder why you are a janitor? I mean you seem well put together and intellectually educated, did something happen or what exactly?" I didn't expect him to answer at all but he smiled and replied, " Well Akeem let me put it this way, sometimes life takes you certain paths you don't want to take but you know you have too because there is something to grasp from that lesson. I do have a college degree, I went to graduate school, and I was living comfortably with what I once did for a living. However, I lost the enjoyment in it, so I stopped. Now I want to go into business with myself, I want to own my own cleaning company. It's not where I want to be right now, but it's a start. "From that brief response to my question, alone, I felt a lot of respect for him. People always say when they don't enjoy their job anymore that they will stop and they usually don't but, for whatever reason, they try prolonging it. He also said, "Life is like a game of soccer, you can run up and down the field as much as you want, but, without a goal, you are just running." Lessons like these can't be learned in the classroom. Mr. E reminded me that life is too short to hang on to what doesn't make you happy. Don't just run around with no goals, you won't get anywhere when you're simply just running.

Chapter Nine - How bad do you want it?

Is this something that you really want? Or is it just something that sounds nice when you say it? Don't say you want better if you're not willing to make the change. Don't tell people what you're doing if you're not actually living it. At some point you need to say enough is enough and get yourself out of a place you don't want to be. Feeling pity for yourself doesn't benefit you, complaining day in and day out doesn't benefit you. Being bitter doesn't benefit you. What benefits you is realizing that there are many possibilities to choose from, and many opportunities for you to bridge the gap between where you are and where you want to be. It's not what you lose along the way that counts, it's what you do with what you still have. Life isn't meant for suffering, there is much more to see and do and you won't be able to get to those things if you're constantly looking down, constantly seeking reactions from people who could care less about you. Don't blame anyone for where you are, it's your life. Trying to avoid responsibility is one of the biggest mistakes we make because every action has a consequence. Before you claim you want better for yourself, make sure that you are willing to do the work to get better.

Stay In Your Lane

All you can do is control what you do, you can't control what anybody else is doing. You need to stay focused on what you're doing. Distractions come from all angles, but if you feed too much into them, you may lose sight of what you're supposed to be doing. It won't always be easy. Sometimes I would see people have success that I know did not work as hard as I do, but yet they would have all the breaks go their way, and for a good amount of time, it would hurt and sometimes I'd want to just give up. It's only human to get fed up when you're working hard for something and you're doing all the right things and still you don't get what's supposed to be coming to you. But over time, I realized that God has a different plan for me just like he has a different plan for everyone. Some people shine now and some people shine later, but eventually everyone will have a time to shine. When it's your time, make the most of it, and enjoy it. When you work hard for what you want, the feeling of accomplishment will open new emotions and make you truly appreciate the process that much more. But what you will remember most will be the pain, tears, heartache that you endured to get to that point. Success is temporary, memories last a lifetime. Stays focused and keep fighting until your time to shine is here.

Start Fighting Back

You can't have a sense of victory unless you know what it means to fail. How you react is the most important rebuttal, waiting to receive what's coming to you is your best bet to fail. Time doesn't wait for anyone, what makes you think it's going to wait for you? Get out and make some things happen for yourself. Be diligent at your work, and stay ready so you won't have to get ready when it's time to make some moves. If you're in a boxing ring with Mike Tyson, and you can win a million dollar prize, but, in order to win, you must consider two options: option one - last the round with him and you win a million dollars, option two - land five punches and you win a million dollars. Which option are you going to take? Me, personally, I'm going to take option two because I know I have a better chance landing five punches then lasting the round, so I'm going out swinging and I'm swinging as long as I'm standing. You can spend a lifetime running away trying to avoid hits and not throwing any yourself or you can fight back and give yourself a fighting chance at being successful. It's on you.

Dealing with Setbacks

It was about 4 PM and I just came home from school and saw my mom sitting on the steps, her eyes looked red and puffy which only meant that she was crying. I asked her what was wrong and she told me that they cut off everything: heat, electricity, water, everything. My mom worked three jobs at the time and she got laid off two of them because the company was declining and couldn't afford to keep too many people. As she explained that to me, all I could do was just stare blankly. My first thought wasn't about me, it was about my two year old brother. He wasn't used to any of this, whereas my mother and I have been through these situations plenty of times. We didn't have anything for about a week, but we made it work. I would walk to my friend's house and heat up my brother's milk and jog back before it became cold. My mom would work her night shift even though she didn't want to leave us alone, but I would tell her to go, it would be fine. Those nights with my little brother were some of the most challenging nights in my life, I didn't want my brother going through the things I had to go through and that hurt me, but I know It hurt my mom even more because she went through that same road with me once before. At nights he would ask me " "Keem where are the lights?" I told him that we were playing a game and mom wanted us not to cheat so she turned off the lights. Immediately after that he said, "If I win, will you buy me games?" My little brother is a strong kid, I admire him for overcoming all he's had in his short life, from almost dying at birth to being admitted in the hospital almost every other week because of sicknesses. "Of course I'll buy you games," I said. Hiding from the inevitable is impossible. Setbacks are going to happen whether you like it or not, it's a part of life that's just how it is and how it will always be. Nobody wants to be down and out, or get hurt, or be lost, but it happens. We can't always help what life throws at us. Sometimes we just have to accept the circumstance for what it is and make the best of it, but we can't give up and throw in the towel. There's a lesson to be learned from every rough situation. When you've dealt with the worst of the worst, what can possible hurt you next? You've already dealt with the worst outcome, so you have no choice but to go up from there. Everyone has as story to tell, every great story gets better when you have some pain that comes out of it. Keep fighting until that pain makes you smile, because you were able to get through what you thought you couldn't.

It's Ok To Say No

I used to have a hard time saying no, and because
of that, I would get myself into some situations that
I didn't want to be in. The first time I ever left for
college, I remember the last week and I was trying
to say bye to my friends and do some last minute
errands. The problem was that there were only so
many hours in a day, every single day I was
hanging out with someone, two hours here and
two hours there and I would go from one place to
the other. Because of that, I wasn't getting my
errands finished nor did I have time to spend with
my mom and little brother at the time. When I
would try and say no to my friends, they would
say, "I won't get to see you for so long," and I
would continue to say yes and I couldn't get out of

it. When it was time to leave at the end of the week, I saw my mom and brother for probably about five hours that whole week. The point to this story is that you can't go around trying to please everybody because it's impossible, someone will always get the short end of the stick. Trying to please everyone is the easiest way to become unhappy. It's okay to say no, so don't put any pressure on yourself accepting something you don't want to do.

Do What You Have To Do

You don't always want to do it, but, in the end, you do what you have to do. Most things you have to endure to get to where you want to be. The process can have your emotions twisted in so many different ways that you get confused. There is a purpose behind every angle that you take. God's plan will take you in so many different directions you will start to begin questioning what He is really doing, but understand that God will take you the furthest route possible if he feels that it will benefit you. You might not want to take orders from anyone, you might not want to go to a job you hate, you might not want to live where you're living now, but sometimes you have to take a step backwards to see why you want to go forwards in the first place. Keep in mind that your recent position is not your final one. Furthermore, remember the bigger picture, every step in the process has its own requirements and right now, this is what God requires you to do. You are one break through away from seizing an opportunity that will change your life.

Chapter Ten - Holding on to Pain

Holding on to pain and whatever has harmed you is like swallowing poison. It attacks you from the inside and kills you slowly. Eventually it will do so much damage on the inside that it will start to show on the outside. Your attitude will be the first thing to show deterioration, and once your attitude changes, its downhill from there. Don't be a slave of the past, things take time to heal, but your happiness won't wait. Dare to let go of what's holding you back, making you sink. Don't give the power to what hurts you or what made you angry. Nothing or no one else should have the power over you. Once you give away a piece of you to someone who's brought you pain, you leave a piece of you with them as well, a piece of you that you cannot get back, until you're willing to forgive and move on with your life. It won't be easy, but in time it will heal. Being internally happy is much more important than having a grudge towards something that can't be changed.

You never know whose Life Your Impacting

You may never know whose life you're impacting, so be careful of the words you use and the actions you do. When I was in high school, there was this kid and I don't recall his name to this day, but he used to hang by himself. Every day, I would see him at lunch time, sitting down in a corner with his headphones in his ears reading a book. He would be in the same spot doing the same thing every single day, but he would never have food. For a few weeks, I would just glimpse if he was there every time I'd walk by. I, also, made note of the fact that he was on my spare as well(a spare is when you have free time instead of class), so one day I went to get some food down the street from my school and then I went to look for him. I eventually found him sitting on the steps outside of the school in the back entrance, and I went up to him and asked him what his name was and he didn't answer, he just kept his head down and stared blankly. I explained what I've been observing about him for the past few weeks. I said to him "I noticed your always sitting in the corner listening to music on lunch time. But yet you never eat any lunch, I went and got you some food, I want you to take my share as well, along with the extra food in the bag. You don't have to accept it but I hope that you will "I left the paper bag with food in it, along with a twenty dollar bill inside. Then I walked away and 5 minutes later, I went to check on him and he was gone, but so was the food which was the most important thing. The next few days I looked for the kid, but I never saw him. Then one day I was late for my class, and as I turned the corner, the kid was walking in my direction, for the first time I saw him with a smirk on his face and his head wasn't down anymore, he was actually looking up. I went over to him and said hello and he looked up and hugged me. Now I'm not a man of all that affectionate stuff, so it was kind of weird to me, but I knew it was a good sign, I mean hugs are good. I then said, "I never truly introduced myself man, I'm Akeem." Until this day, I remember vividly the next words he said like it happened yesterday, "I know who you are man, everybody knows who you are, I just wanted to say thank you for what you've done. My family has been having some rough times and my parents didn't have much money to give me to eat. I wouldn't have imagined someone like you taking the time to stop and even care about me. Most people don't notice me anyway. You really are as great of a guy as everyone else says. Thank-you. I can't tell you how much that meant to me." I wasn't sure what to say, I was kind of shocked, I don't see myself as any one special, everyone is fighting a battle that we know nothing about, and nobody deserves to go through anything alone. He was only in the 10th grade and since I was graduating in a few months, I knew that I needed to do something more so others would take care of him. Later in the week I introduced him to some people who I knew in his same grade and a grade higher, and I told specific ones to make sure he gets some food and taken care of when i was gone. I didn't have money myself, in fact, the money that I gave him was money that I had for about three weeks that I was trying to make stretch, but I just wanted to help somebody who looked like they needed it. If you can help anyone, it will go a long way, even if it's something small. There is no greater feeling than spreading joy to those who need it.

Critics & Naysayers

Expect people to talk about you and bad mouth
you whenever they have the chance to do so. They
won't remember all the good things you have done
but will be the first to call you out when you've
made a mistake. The best way to deal with this is to
just let them talk and keep watching you learn
about yourself and become better as a whole.
People always forget that everyone makes
mistakes. We are all students of life, and no one is
perfect so why portray it like we are. Without
making mistakes how do you expect anyone to
grow and learn how to deal with the transition of

becoming who we are? Buying too much into what people say is a good start to becoming unhappy. Whether it's something good or bad, someone will always critic your judgments and choices, but that's okay. At the end of the day, it's your life, live your life how you want to live it. Who are they to say what's right from what's wrong. Chances are if they had their life together, they wouldn't be commenting and talking about yours.

Get Comfortable in Your Own Skin

Growing up I was chubby like I said in an earlier chapter, all the foods I used to eat weren't the best for me, but it tasted great, so I ate whatever it was that was prepared. It wasn't until I was about ten –

twelve years old that I started dropping a little

weight because I started playing sports and

becoming active on a daily basis. I still wasn't

happy with how my body looked and for years,

and I became very self-conscious, even when I

started to put on some muscle, I was still not

comfortable. I started eating much better and

became sort of a health freak. I rarely ate anything

junk and what I considered junk was really not

what most would consider junk, it would be a

chocolate milk here or there, a piece of banana

bread. Like I said, it's not what most consider junk,

but I stayed away from mostly anything that

wasn't beneficial. Even until this day I am still very

careful as to what I put in my body. I'm still

working towards my goals, but I am happy in my

own skin. The point to this reflection is that you

don't need any type or surgeries or shots or extremes to make yourself feel good. Eat properly, exercise, and make a routine to stay fit, not only mentally but physically. There is no such thing as the perfect body, but if you're not happy with yourself, make some changes. You don't have to have a six pack or flat stomach to be considered "Fit or Healthy" Although you do need to take care of yourself. If you take care of your body, your body will take care of you.

Three Simple tips to Overpower Negativity

1 -Two Wrongs Don't Make a Right

The first thing you can't do is start being negative to yourself because that's pointless. You won't get anywhere and it only makes you feel worse. Instead, try and find one good thing that happened. When you dwell on negativity, it starts to take a toll on you. It's like stress and when a person is stressed, it shows. Remind yourself that it's going to be alright, it's hard but you must be optimistic. A bad situation won't last forever. It comes to test you even when you're not prepared and least expect it. That's fine, you're more prepared than you think. Just believe it.

2 -People will be people

People may talk about you, people may tell you that they can do better or could have done it better, people may claim they have your back and when push comes to shove they're not there. That's fine. No matter how many people have doubt in you or tell you that you can't do something, do it anyway. You don't need to listen to them, let them talk. They will never know who you really are and they don't need to. When it's your time, your cup will overflow

3 -How Do You Know When It's Your Time?

Well you don't. It's a blessing and a curse. It's a blessing because it keeps you on your toes and pushes you to do better every day. You are one important detail away from doing something great. It's a curse

because you have to wait and play mind games in

your head. It's hard to be positive in a negative world

but it's even harder to fight off the negativity of your

own thoughts in your head. If you can fight off those

thoughts, the rest of the negativity in the world gets

easier.

Whatever we do, we have to be patient.

The biggest misconception people make

about patience is thinking you have to

wait there and do nothing. The biggest

thing is what you are doing while you're

being patient. Are you still doing the right things? Are you still pushing yourself each day? When you make yourself better, you make the people around you better as well.

Closing remarks

I hope this book helped you in any way that it could. I thank you again for taking the time to read this book. I hope you enjoy the road to your success and hopefully something from this book will help you get through those tough days when you feel like quitting. Life is what you make it, so make the best of every single day. If you like the book, be sure to share it. Thank you, God Bless

Chris

Thank ya for all that you do,
Truly appreciate it and I know
i'm not the only one.
   Hope you Enjoy the Book

Made in the USA
Charleston, SC
03 October 2016